# First World War
### and Army of Occupation
# War Diary
### France, Belgium and Germany

52 DIVISION
Divisional Troops
Divisional Cyclist Company
1 April 1918 - 4 May 1918

WO95/2892/1

The Naval & Military Press Ltd
www.nmarchive.com
**Published in association with The National Archives**

Published by

## The Naval & Military Press Ltd

Unit 10 Ridgewood Industrial Park,

Uckfield, East Sussex,

TN22 5QE England

Tel: +44 (0) 1825 749494

www.naval-military-press.com

www.nmarchive.com

*This diary has been reprinted in facsimile from the original. Any imperfections are inevitably reproduced and the quality may fall short of modern type and cartographic standards.*

**© Crown Copyright**
**Images reproduced by permission of The National Archives, London, England, 2015.**

# Contents

| Document type | Place/Title | Date From | Date To |
|---|---|---|---|
| Heading | WO95/2892/1 Divisional Cyclist Company | | |
| Heading | 52nd Division 52nd Divl Coy Army Cyclist Corps Apr-May 1918 | | |
| War Diary | Z 28.d | 01/04/1918 | 01/04/1918 |
| War Diary | S.20.C | 02/04/1918 | 07/04/1918 |
| War Diary | Kantara Egypt | 07/04/1918 | 08/04/1918 |
| War Diary | Sidi Bishr | 09/04/1918 | 18/04/1918 |
| War Diary | At Sea | 19/04/1918 | 27/04/1918 |
| War Diary | In The Train | 28/04/1918 | 30/04/1918 |
| Miscellaneous | Herewith War Diary Of Late 52nd Divisional Cyclist Coy | 23/05/1918 | 23/05/1918 |
| War Diary | Buigny St. Maclou | 01/05/1918 | 04/05/1918 |

W095/2892/1
Dursoronal Cyclist Company

## 52ND DIVISION

52ND DIVL COY.
ARMY ~~CATERING~~ CYCLIST CORPS
APR-MAY 1918

# WAR DIARY or INTELLIGENCE SUMMARY

Army Form C. 2118.

Folio 17. Vol III

52nd DIVISIONAL COY A.G.C.

| Place | Date | Hour | Summary of Events and Information | Remarks and references to Appendices |
|---|---|---|---|---|
| Z28.d. | 1.4.18 | | **Routine** Reveille 0530, Breakfast 0630 (until 11.00 Branches 17.00. | PALESTINE EXPLORATION FUND MAP SHEET XIII |
| | | | **Duties** Upon receipt of instructions from XXIst Corps - Men were 9602 d/3/9/6 arrangements were made to relieve all duties supplied by Coy. The following reported the unit:- | supplied by Coy. |
| STRENGTH OF COMPANY AS SHOWN IN PART II ORDERS 21/4/18 | | | 6 ORs from Headquarters XXIst Corps<br>1/Lieut W.H. ORR from A.D.S.T. XXIst Corps<br>10 ORs from B.A.D.A.R.S. XXIst Corps<br>2/Lt POTTER, 2/Lt WEBER and 2 ORs from XXIst Corps Detail Camp.<br>2/Lt LAPP & 4 ORs from A.D.S.T. XXIst Corps | List. |
| Officers 13 | | | All Guards, Headquarters (XXIst Corps) orderlies & Regtal. Railway and traffic control posts, were relieved in this day. | List. |
| C.S.M. 1 | | | | |
| C.Q.M.S. 1 | | | **Move** The Company paraded at 17.30 with cycles and moved to SURAFEND during the night 1st/2nd April. In accordance with XXIst Corps order 9602 d/3/5/6 which was in support | |
| Sergeants 4 | | | | |
| L.Sgts 2 | | | | |
| Cpls 17 | | | | |
| L/Cpls 15 | | | | |
| 1 Cpk 1 | | | | |
| 2 Cpk 1 | | | "52 Div Cyclist Coy will move to SURAFEND area after dark on April 1st 2nd where they will come under orders of GOC 52nd Div A.D.A. 52 Div will arrange bivouac area etc." | |
| Bands 252 | | | The Company marched to their camping area 520.c. at 24.00. During the movements of other troops along the SURAFEND Road the march to the bivouac was frequently delayed. Cycling being almost impossible. | |
| Total 311 | | | | |
| | | | | |
| S20.c. | 2.4.18 | | **Routine** As for 1st inst. - Lights Out 21.00. | |
| | | | Two ORs attached for lorry duty returned to 208 ASC M.T. from Coy. to Hospital | |

2353 Wt. W2514/1454 700,000 5/15 D. D. & L. A.D.S.S./Forms/C. 2118.

# WAR DIARY
## or
## INTELLIGENCE SUMMARY.
(Erase heading not required.)

Army Form C. 2118.

Folio 18
Vol II
52nd DIVISIONAL Equipment Coy A.O.C.

| Place | Date | Hour | Summary of Events and Information | Remarks and references to Appendices |
|---|---|---|---|---|
| S 20 c | 3.4.18 | | Routine. Reveille 0630, Breakfast 0630, Teas 1000, Dinners 1730, Lights out 21.00. Coy cycles in possession of the Company were returned to Ordnance, LUDD under 52nd Div A.O.M Ins No 16, Para 6, together with harness, & a portion of Latrine equipment. | PALESTINE EXPLORATION FUND MAP SHEET XIII. Nil |
| | 4.4.18 | | Routine as for 3rd inst. Paraded. The Company paraded at 0915 for care of Boy Respirators and then after proceeded to 52 DV stables by Gnr Rail to Ordnance shops & LUDD Station. | Nil |
| | 5.4.18 | | Routine as for 4th inst — Paraded. The Company paraded for care of Barrack Sheds-y & inspection of Box Respirators | Nil |
| | 6.4.18 | | Routine as for 5th inst. Scapts Rest. Dinners 12.00 Teas 16.00 More. Barrow chests returned to A.O.D. SURAFEND. All other stores not accompanying the Coy were returned to Ordnance LUDD. Vide 52nd Div A.O.M, Ins Para 7. The Company paraded at 21.30 and marched to LUDD Station. Entraining was completed at 22.00 | Nil |
| | 7.4.18 | | Routine. Teas 18.30 Lights out 21.30 More. The Company moved away by train from LUDD Station at 02.05, EL ARISH, was reached at 11.00 – 20 mm halt and arrived at KANTARA. EAST at 17.30 after detraining the Company was marched to No 1 Base Depot- MA-KANTARA and men hurriedly on details in tents. One o.r. to Hospital. | Nil |
| KANTARA EGYPT. | | | | |

Army Form C. 2118.

Folio 19.
Vol III.
52nd Divisional Coy A.C.C.

# WAR DIARY
## or
## INTELLIGENCE SUMMARY.
(Erase heading not required.)

Instructions regarding War Diaries and Intelligence Summaries are contained in F. S. Regs., Part II. and the Staff Manual respectively. Title pages will be prepared in manuscript.

| Place | Date | Hour | Summary of Events and Information | Remarks and references to Appendices |
|---|---|---|---|---|
| KANTARA EGYPT | 8.4.18 | | **Routine** Reveille 0600, Breakfast 7.00, Teas 12.00, Dinners 1600. On instructions from the A.O.D KANTARA. 53 O.R.'s ADM INS N6 para 10. The following clothing and equipment was drawn and issued to the Company: Knickerbockers Cyclist, Shirt Khaki's Clothing and Boots. Used replacements were exchanged for new articles. | Nil |
| | | | **PARADES** The Company paraded at 18.45" and marched to KANTARA West Station. Entrainment was completed 2030 and the Train left the Station at 2130. LT DIXON to Hospital | |
| S.I.O.I. B.S.N.R. | 9.4.18 | | **Routine** Teas 1200. Dinners 1700. Lights Out 2130. The Company arrived by train at S.I.O.I. B.S.N.R. at 0730, were marched to the Transit Camp and accommodated in Tents | Nil |
| | 10.4.18 | | **Routine** Reveille 0600. Breakfast 0700. Teas 1200. Dinners 1600. **Duties** The following duties were found by the Company: 2 Sergeants in the O.R's Station Piquet. 2 Guards of 1 N.C.O. & 6 O.R's for duties at the Grocery & Wet Canteen. | Nil |
| | 11.4.18 | | **Routine & Duties** as for 10th inst. **Parades** A Fatigue Party of 1 Officer and 100 O.R.s reported for work under the Camp. Q.M. The Company paraded for pay at 1100 | Nil |

2353 Wt. W2544/1454 700,000 5/15 D.D.&L. A.D.S.S./Forms/C. 2118.

Army Form C. 2118.

Folio 20
Vol III
53rd DIVISIONAL Coy A.C.C.

# WAR DIARY
## or
## INTELLIGENCE SUMMARY.
(Erase heading not required.)

Instructions regarding War Diaries and Intelligence Summaries are contained in F. S. Regs., Part II. and the Staff Manual respectively. Title pages will be prepared in manuscript.

| Place | Date | Hour | Summary of Events and Information | Remarks and references to Appendices |
|---|---|---|---|---|
| SIDI BISHR. | 12.4.18 | | Routine. Reveille 0600 Breakfasts 0700 Teas 1500 Dinners 1600 Lights Out. 21/30 Parades. The Company paraded 0630-0700 for Running Drill. | nil. |
| | 13.4.18 | | Routine & Parades as for 12th inst. Duties. The Company supplied the following detail:— Lying Regt. 1 Officer and 50 OR. Pierce Regt. One Sergeant and 12 OR. Two OR. to Hospital. One OR. from Trade Test. | nil |
| | 14.4.18 | | Routine as for 13th inst. Parades. The Company tear R.C. paraded for Divine Service at 0900 at the Camp Chapel — Albert Hoar. | nil |
| | 15.4.18 | | Routine as for 14th inst. Parades. The Company paraded 0630-0700 for Running Drill, and for Sea Bathing at 1000. Duties. The Company supplied the following duties. Tram Piquet 2 Sergeants & 24 OR. Officers Mess Piquet 1 " & 6 OR. One OR. from Hospital. | nil |
| | 16.4.18 | | Routine & Parades as for 15th inst. Bathing as for 15th inst. | nil |
| | 17.4.18 | | Routine and Parades as for 16th inst. Instructions were received for 2/Lt. V.B. APPLETON to Report for Instruction at KANTARA with a view to transfer to the R.A.F. Two OR. to Hospital. | nil |

# WAR DIARY
## or
## INTELLIGENCE SUMMARY.
*(Erase heading not required.)*

Army Form C. 2118.

Folio 21.
Vol. III
52nd DIVISIONAL Coy ACC

| Place | Date | Hour | Summary of Events and Information | Remarks and references to Appendices |
|---|---|---|---|---|
| SIDI BISHR | 18.4.18 | | **Routine.** Reveille 0600. Breakfast 0700.<br>**Move.** The Company entrained at Sidi Bishr Station at 0930 and proceeded to the Quay Side ALEXANDRIA DOCKS. Men and baggage embarked on H.M.T. MENOMINEE by 1300 –<br>**Duties.** The following permanent duty fatigues were appointed by the Company for the voyage.<br>Ship's Adjutant. Captain IW McDougal<br>Quarter Master. Lt. R.C. Leslie<br>"Sergeant" C.Q.M.S. Aitcheson<br>"Sergeant" L/Sgt. Forrest<br>Provost Sergeant. 2/Lt. E.J. Potter<br>Officers of the watch. 2/Lt. V. Weber<br>Water fatigue. 1 Sgt and 21 ORs<br>Deck fatigue. 1 Cpl " 12 "<br>The Transport moved away from the Quay at 1600 and dropped anchor in the outer harbour. | Nil. |
| AT SEA | 19.4.18 | | **Routine.** Reveille 0530 Breakfast 0730. Dinners 1230 Teas 1700 No lights after dark.<br>The Transport left port at 1600.<br>Strength of Company proceeding Overseas<br>9 Officers 219 ORs | Nil. |
| " | 20.4.18 | | **Routine** as for 19th instant.<br>**Parade.** The Company paraded daily at 1000 hrs when inspected by O.C. Ships.<br>The weather was fine and the sea calm during the voyage. | Nil. |

Army Form C. 2118.

# WAR DIARY
## or
## INTELLIGENCE SUMMARY.

(Erase heading not required.)

FOLIO 22.
Vol. 4.
52nd DIVISIONAL CYCLIST COY

Instructions regarding War Diaries and Intelligence Summaries are contained in F. S. Regs., Part II. and the Staff Manual respectively. Title pages will be prepared in manuscript.

| Place | Date | Hour | Summary of Events and Information | Remarks and references to Appendices |
|---|---|---|---|---|
| AT SEA. | 27.4.16 | Reveille | Reveille 0630. Breakfast 0700. Dinner 1230. Tea 1600. The Transport arrived at MARSEILLES, FRANCE and anchored at the Quay side at 1100. The Company disembarked at 1700 and entrained at the Quay side Station at 21.00. One OR to Hospital. | Nil. |
| IN THE TRAIN | 28.4.16 | Routine | Breakfast and rations issued at LE TEIL at 10.00 Tea issued at PARAY-LE-MONIAL at 22.00 | Nil |
|  | 29.4.16 | Routine | Breakfast and rations carried at MALESHERBES 10.19. Two other stops made during the day at any station where Tea could be obtained. | Nil |
|  | 30.4.16 | | The Company detrained at NOYELLES at 10.00. A hot meal was issued at the Transit Camp adjoining the station. Baggage etc sent forward by motor lorry to BUIGNY. ST. MACLOU. The Company paraded at 12.00 & took march order and proceeded to march to BUIGNY. ST. MACLOU where all ranks were billeted in the houses and barns of the village. Tea 18.00 Lights 21.00. | REF. MAP. FRANCE. ABBEVILLE Sheet 14. |
|  | | Strength. | The Company embarked Khaki at its above strength - less one OR of which Ken left Egypt. i.e. 9 Officers 218 ORs | Nil |

Signed [signature]
Captain,
Commanding 52nd Divisional Coy.

D.A.A.G. I. 24

Herewith War Diary of late 52nd Divisional Cyclist Coy, completed to date on which this Unit was disbanded, i.e., 4/5/18.

23/5/18

[signature] Lieut for
O/c No 5 Infantry Section
G.H.Q. 3rd Echelon

TRACT FORM.   20 MAY 1918        Army Form W3391.

| Name. | Date of Admission. | Casualty. | Remarks. |
|---|---|---|---|
| rcival W | 11/5 | Gnt Shy L R | Remy |
| elsmore Ja | ? | 6tk wda | 11/5 Base 8 |

**WAR DIARY** or **INTELLIGENCE SUMMARY**
Army Form C. 2118.

52nd Divisional Coy. ACC

Vol. VII   Folio 73

| Place | Date | Hour | Summary of Events and Information | Remarks and references to Appendices |
|---|---|---|---|---|
| BUIGNY ST. MACLOU | 1.5.18 | | Routine: Reveille 0600 Breakfast 0730 Dinners 1230 Teas 1700 Lights Out 2100. | |
| | | | Parades: Coy paraded for Inspector of Iron Rations at their Alarm Posts. Completion 10.30. 1 O.R. to Hospital. | |
| | 2.5.18 | | Routine: As usual. | |
| | | | Parades: Coy. Paraded for Running Drill 0630 – 0700. 2 O.R. to Hospital. | |
| | 3.5.18 | | Routine: As usual. | |
| | | | Parades: Coy. paraded for Running Drill 0615 – 0645. " " " " Steady " 0930 – 1130. Inspections of Clothing etc. carried out by Coy. Officers. Steady Drill Parade. Provisional orders were received for villages piquets from Beerne Army. The following Wire Q 300 d/2.5.18. "You will proceed tomorrow by Rail to ROUEN reporting on arrival to CYCLIST BASE DEPOT MAN " " " Train leaves 10.50 p.m. M.R. Entraining Station NOYELLES SUR MER AAA | |

2353  Wt. W2544/1454 700,000 5/15 D.D.&L. AD.S.S./Form/C. 2118.

Army Form C. 2118.

# WAR DIARY
## or
## INTELLIGENCE SUMMARY.
(Erase heading not required.)

Folio 24.

Vol III. 52nd Divl Coy. A.C.C.

| Place | Date | Hour | Summary of Events and Information | Remarks and references to Appendices |
|---|---|---|---|---|
| BUGNY ST MARTIN | 3.5.18 | | "A.D.S.T. will arrange for two days rations for 279 all ranks to be dumped under guard at NOYELLES Station by 7.30 pm Tomorrow AAA Five rations will be handed over to O.C. CYCLISTS and taken in train AAA Personnel will be at entraining Station one hour before train is due to leave AAA A.D.S.T. will also detail one lorry to report to Headquarters Cyclist Coy. BUGNY at 2:30 pm tomorrow to convey kits to station AAA Adv 52nd Divl Cyc. Coy. Reprsts A.D.S.T. AAA". The following memo was also received from Reserve Army:— "In view of the ruling in G.H.Q. letter 08/3109 of 24th April that the 52nd Divl Cyclist Coy. will be taken as reinforcements, the equipment of this unit will be dealt with as follows:— "1 Personal equipment, arms, accoutrements, steel helmets & box respirators will be retained. "The containers of the box respirators will be changed for the N.C. (New) containers where these are not already in possession. "Blankets will be made up to 2 per man and this number will be retained by the men. "2 All Regimental Equipment will be returned to Ordnance Base Depot." | [signature] |

Army Form C. 2118.

# WAR DIARY
## or
## INTELLIGENCE SUMMARY.
(Erase heading not required.)

52nd Divisional Cyc. Coy.

Vol. III.    Folio 25

| Place | Date | Hour | Summary of Events and Information | Remarks and references to Appendices |
|---|---|---|---|---|
| BUSIGNY | 4.5.18 | | The Coy. paraded Full Marching Order at 1800 & proceeded to Royelles for entraining. | |
| ST. MARTIN | | | The Coy. entrained at NOYELLES at 1700 arrived at ROUEN at 0300 for ROUEN. DEPOT with stores baggage. Proceeded to CYCLIST BASE was taken over by CYCLIST BASE DEPOT for the purpose of general reinforcements under the authority above mentioned. This completes the War Diary of the 52nd Divnl. Cyclist Coy. | |

[Signature]
Commanding 52nd Divnl. Cyclist Corps.

52ND DIVISIONAL C[OY]
No.
Date 4.5.18
ARMY CYCLIST CORPS

(A8004) D. D. & L., London, E.C. Wt. W1771/M2131 750,000 5/17  Sch. 52  Forms/C2118/14

www.ingramcontent.com/pod-product-compliance
Lightning Source LLC
Chambersburg PA
CBHW081513160426
43193CB00014B/2678